T0124903

tiny book of.

CHRISTMAS JOY

tiny book of
CHRISTMAS JOY

Recipes *and* Inspiration *for the* Holidays

Small Pleasures™
· SERIES ·

hm | books

Small Pleasures
• SERIES •
hm | books

PRESIDENT *Phyllis Hoffman DePiano*
PRESIDENT/CCO *Brian Hart Hoffman*
VICE PRESIDENT/EDITORIAL *Cindy Smith Cooper*
ART DIRECTOR *Jodi Rankin Daniels*
COPY EDITORS *Whitney Durrwachter, Avery Hurt*
CREATIVE DIRECTOR/PHOTOGRAPHY *Mac Jamieson*
SENIOR PHOTOGRAPHERS
John O'Hagan, Marcy Black Simpson
PHOTOGRAPHERS *Jim Bathie, William Dickey,*
Stephanie Welbourne
TEST KITCHEN PROFESSIONALS
Allene Arnold, Kathleen Kanen, Janet Lambert,
Vanessa Rocchio, Anna Theoktisto, Loren Wood
TEST KITCHEN ASSISTANT *Anita Simpson Spain*
SENIOR DIGITAL IMAGING SPECIALIST *Delisa McDaniel*
DIGITAL IMAGING SPECIALIST *Clark Densmore*

hm

CHAIRMAN OF THE BOARD/CEO *Phyllis Hoffman DePiano*
PRESIDENT/COO *Eric W. Hoffman*
PRESIDENT/CCO *Brian Hart Hoffman*
EXECUTIVE VICE PRESIDENT/CFO *Mary P. Cummings*
EXECUTIVE VICE PRESIDENT/O&M *Greg Baugh*
VICE PRESIDENT/DIGITAL MEDIA *Jon Adamson*
VICE PRESIDENT/EDITORIAL *Cindy Smith Cooper*
VICE PRESIDENT/ADMINISTRATION *Lynn Lee Terry*

Hoffman Media
1900 International Park Drive, Suite 50
Birmingham, Alabama 35243
www.hoffmanmedia.com

ISBN # 978-1-940772-22-6
Printed in China

ON THE COVER: (Front) Peppermint-Mocha Brownies, page 36. (Back) Creamy Peppermint Punch, page 19. Photography by Marcy Black Simpson. Recipe development and food styling by Kathleen Kanen.

Contents

INTRODUCTION

The joy of Christmas comes once a year with special traditions and gifts to give. Those wonderful hours spent with family and friends will be cherished for years to come.

– PHYLLIS HOFFMAN DEPIANO

LET THE CHRISTMAS MAGIC begin with the true meaning of Christmas. Within this little book, we give you a collection of delicious and beautifully photographed recipes along with lots of entertaining and decorating ideas to help you spread the holiday spirit with minimum stress and lots of memorable time with family and friends. From greetings and hugs at the front door to caroling in the neighborhood, from festive wreaths to hostess gifts, your holidays can be both pleasurable and relaxing.

In the opening pages, "Christmas Inspiration," you'll find teas and warm beverages as well as quick ideas for wreaths, mantels, and stairways that will get family and guests in the holiday mood as soon as they step through your door. The chapter "Hosting Guests" provides plenty of easy caroling recipes and quick divine desserts and candies to share with your guests, whether a couple or a crowd. "Handmade Gifts" completes the book with clever mixes, candies, and jams—and of course, unique wrapping ideas.

I've also sprinkled in a few inspirational quotes and some of my own comments, tips, and cherished memories. I hope this selection of traditional favorites will make planning the season easier than ever. Once your work is done, put on your holiday clothes and watch for the man in the red suit with the sleigh!

Christmas Inspiration

THE SCENTS AND SMELLS WAFTING FROM
THE KITCHEN DRAW GUESTS INSIDE AND
SAY 'WELCOME.' WARM BEVERAGES ALONG
WITH IDEAS FOR SIMPLE DECORATING INVITE
ONE AND ALL COME IN AND VISIT.

Hot Spiced Cider

8 cups apple cider
12 whole allspice
12 whole cloves
3 cinnamon sticks
1 vanilla bean, split
    lengthwise and
    scraped
Brandy (optional)
Garnish: cinnamon sticks

In a large Dutch oven, combine cider, allspice, cloves, cinnamon sticks, and vanilla bean and seeds. Simmer for 30 minutes to 1 hour. Remove from heat; strain and discard solids. Pour hot cider into mugs, and add 1 to 2 tablespoons brandy per serving, if desired. Garnish with cinnamon sticks, if desired.

Christmas is the day that holds all time together.

– ALEXANDER SMITH

CLASSIC EGGNOG
page 15

GINGERBREAD COOKIES
page 16

ome, let us

Classic Eggnog

In a large saucepan, whisk together milk, half-and-half, sugar, eggs, vanilla, and salt. Bring just to a boil over medium-high heat, whisking constantly until thickened. Immediately pour into a serving bowl. Stir in cinnamon and nutmeg. Cover, and chill until ready to serve. Stir in bourbon. Serve with a cinnamon stick and a sprinkle of nutmeg, if desired.

NONALCOHOLIC VERSION In a large saucepan, whisk together 2¼ cups milk, half-and-half, sugar, eggs, vanilla, and salt. Bring just to a boil over medium high heat, whisking constantly until thickened. Immediately pour into serving bowl. Stir in cinnamon and nutmeg. Cover, and chill until ready to serve. Stir in remaining 1 cup milk. Serve with a cinnamon stick and a sprinkle of nutmeg, if desired.

MAKES 10 SERVINGS

2¼ cups whole milk, divided
2/3 cup half-and-half
3/4 cup sugar
6 large eggs, beaten
1 teaspoon vanilla extract
¼ teaspoon salt
¼ teaspoon ground cinnamon
¼ teaspoon ground nutmeg
3/4 cup bourbon
Garnish: cinnamon stick, ground nutmeg

NONALCOHOLIC VERSION
MAKES 10 SERVINGS

3¼ cups whole milk, divided
2/3 cup half-and-half
3/4 cup sugar
6 large eggs, beaten
1 teaspoon vanilla extract
¼ teaspoon salt
¼ teaspoon ground cinnamon
¼ teaspoon ground nutmeg
Garnish: cinnamon stick, ground nutmeg

Gingerbread Cookies

Preheat oven to 350°. Line baking sheets with parchment paper.

In a small saucepan, bring shortening, sugar, molasses, and vinegar to a boil over high heat. Remove from heat, and let cool; whisk in egg.

In a large bowl, combine flour, baking soda, cinnamon, ginger, salt, nutmeg, and cloves. Stir in molasses mixture. Cover, and chill overnight.

On a lightly floured surface, roll dough to ¼-inch thickness. Using a house-shaped cookie cutter, cut out dough. Place 1 inch apart on prepared baking sheets. Bake for 10 minutes. Let cool on pans for 2 minutes. Remove from pans, and cool completely on wire racks.

In a large bowl, beat confectioners' sugar, milk, and vanilla until blended. Spoon frosting into a squeeze bottle or pastry bag, and decorate cookies.

MAKES ABOUT 21 COOKIES

- ½ cup all-vegetable shortening
- ⅓ cup sugar
- ½ cup molasses
- 1½ teaspoons vinegar
- 1 large egg, beaten
- 3 cups all-purpose flour
- ½ teaspoon baking soda
- ½ teaspoon ground cinnamon
- ½ teaspoon ground ginger
- ¼ teaspoon salt
- ⅛ teaspoon ground nutmeg
- ⅛ teaspoon ground cloves
- 2 cups confectioners' sugar
- 2½ tablespoons whole milk
- 1 teaspoon vanilla extract

Creamy Peppermint Punch

In a large punch bowl, combine softened ice cream, half-and-half, sparkling water, and extract; stir well. Moisten the edges of serving glasses with water, and dip in red sugar, if desired. Add punch to glasses; garnish with a candy cane and crushed peppermints, if desired.

MAKES ABOUT 20 SERVINGS

1 gallon vanilla ice cream, softened
2 cups half-and-half
2 cups sparkling water, chilled
1 tablespoon peppermint extract, or to taste
Garnish: red sanding sugar, peppermint candy canes, finely crushed peppermints

Be sure and treat guests to the sweet sensation of the holiday's favorite candy. There is nothing like the taste of peppermint to recall the joys of Christmas.

– PHYLLIS HOFFMAN DEPIANO

Sweet & Spicy
Ham & Turkey Sliders

MAKES 24 SERVINGS

2 (12-ounce) packages
    Hawaiian rolls
½ cup butter
2 tablespoons grated
    onion
2 tablespoons seeded
    and chopped
    jalapeño peppers
2 tablespoons harvest
    ground mustard
1 teaspoon sugar
1 teaspoon
    Worcestershire sauce
1 tablespoon sesame
    seeds
¾ pound thinly sliced
    smoked ham
¾ pound thinly sliced
    smoked turkey
6 slices Havarti cheese

Preheat oven to 350°.

Without separating rolls, slice rolls horizontally. Set aside.

In a small saucepan, combine butter, onion, jalapeños, mustard, sugar, and Worcestershire sauce. Cook over medium heat for 5 to 8 minutes, or until butter is melted and onion is translucent. Stir in sesame seeds.

Brush melted butter mixture on cut sides of rolls. Layer ham, turkey, and Havarti on bottoms of rolls. Top with remaining rolls. Brush tops with butter mixture. Wrap rolls in aluminum foil. Bake for 15 minutes, or until cheese is melted.

CHOCOLATE DIPPED
MARSHMALLOWS
page 24

Hot Cocoa

In a large bowl, whisk together cocoa powders, confectioners' sugar, nondairy creamer, cinnamon, salt, and nutmeg until well blended. Stir 3 to 4 tablespoons cocoa mixture into 1 cup hot milk for each serving. Serve immediately.

MAKES APPROXIMATELY 20 SERVINGS

1 cup unsweetened cocoa powder*
½ cup special dark cocoa powder*
3 cups confectioners' sugar
1 cup nondairy creamer
1 teaspoon ground cinnamon
1 teaspoon salt
¼ teaspoon ground nutmeg

*We used Hershey's Natural Unsweetened Cocoa Powder and Hershey's Special Dark Cocoa Powder.

Holiday Houseplant

Hang a few ornaments from a favorite houseplant to make a festive centerpiece that costs little to nothing. Place a few more ornaments to cover the topsoil and you're finished. So easy.

Chocolate-Dipped Marshmallows

Makes 2 dozen
marshmallows

**24 (4-inch) lollipop
sticks**
24 marshmallows
**1 pound chocolate-
flavored candy
coating**

Line 2 baking sheets with wax paper; set aside.

Place lollipop sticks in marshmallows. Melt candy coating according to package directions. Dip marshmallows into candy coating halfway up the sides, allowing excess to drip off. Place on prepared pans, and cool until set. Store in an airtight container at room temperature for up to 3 days.

The Christmas Countdown
Plan ahead for holiday entertaining with these easy ideas.

A week ahead: Make grocery list and purchase nonperishable items.

Two to three days ahead: Decide on china, drink ware, serving dishes, and silverware. Plan any table decorations, entry garlands, and wreaths. Prepare cookies or other make-ahead items and store in air tight containers. Purchase perishable items.

One day ahead: Prepare any dips or sauces and chill. Prepare any make-ahead casseroles or dishes, cakes, and pies.

Day of celebration: Prepare any fresh vegetables or casseroles. Cook meats the day you'll serve them, unless they're precooked and only require warming. Prepare salads and fresh fruits, and chill.

Half hour to hour before guests arrive: Warm foods and light candles. Brew coffee and prepare warm beverages as needed.

Mulled Pomegranate Cider

In a large saucepan, combine juice, wine, honey, cloves, cinnamon sticks, and pears. Cook, uncovered, for 30 minutes over medium heat (do not let mixture boil). Add pear nectar, stirring to combine. Serve warm or chilled.

MAKES ABOUT 1 GALLON

- **8 cups pomegranate juice**
- **1 (750-milliliter) bottle red wine**
- **¼ cup honey**
- **5 whole cloves**
- **2 cinnamon sticks**
- **1 red pear, seeded and sliced**
- **1 green pear, seeded and sliced**
- **4 cups pear nectar**

Come Christmas Eve, we usually go to my mom and dad's. Everybody brings one gift and then we play that game when we all steal it from each other. Some are really cool, others are useful, and some are a bit out there.

– AMY GRANT

Old-Fashioned Hot Chocolate

4 cups heavy whipping cream, divided
2 tablespoons vanilla extract, divided
1/3 cup confectioners' sugar
3 cups half-and-half
3/4 cup bourbon
1/4 cup almond-flavored liqueur
2 (10.5-ounce) packages hot cocoa mix*
1 tablespoon orange zest
Garnish: whipped cream, chocolate curls

We used Ghirardelli Double Chocolate Hot Cocoa.

In a large bowl, beat 2 cups cream, 1 tablespoon vanilla, and confectioners' sugar with a mixer at high speed until medium peaks form. Cover, and chill until ready to use.

In a medium saucepan, combine half-and-half, next 2 ingredients, remaining 2 cups cream, and remaining 1 tablespoon vanilla. Bring to a boil over medium-high heat; reduce heat to medium. Whisk in cocoa mix. Remove from heat. Fold in reserved whipped cream and orange zest. Garnish with whipped cream and chocolate curls, if desired.

Create a kissing ball by soaking a round floral foam ball in water until completely wet. Wrap a piece of chicken wire around it and tie on a piece of ribbon for hanging. Insert fresh evergreens and mistletoe. Hang in a doorway.

– PHYLLIS HOFFMAN DEPIANO

Loaded Potato Soup

In a large Dutch oven or stockpot, cook bacon over medium heat until crisp; remove bacon, and crumble, reserving 3 tablespoons drippings in pan. Cook green onion in bacon drippings for 1 to 2 minutes or until tender. Stir in flour, and cook for 1 minute, stirring constantly. Gradually add chicken broth, whisking constantly, until smooth. Add potatoes, salt, and pepper. Bring to a boil. Reduce heat to medium-low; simmer, uncovered, for 20 minutes, stirring occasionally. Whisk in buttermilk and sour cream. Add cheese, stirring until cheese is melted. Garnish with cheese, chopped green onion, and reserved crumbled bacon, if desired.

MAKES 10 TO 12 SERVINGS

1 (1-pound) package sliced applewood-smoked bacon
1 bunch green onions, chopped
3/4 cup all-purpose flour
3 quarts low-sodium chicken broth
6 cups diced Yukon gold potatoes
6 cups diced red potatoes
1 teaspoon salt
1/2 teaspoon ground black pepper
2 cups whole buttermilk
1 cup sour cream
4 cups shredded sharp Cheddar cheese
Garnish: shredded Cheddar cheese, chopped green onion, bacon

Cranberry Tonic

MAKES 8 SERVINGS

1 cup sugar
1 cup water
¼ cup chopped fresh
rosemary
¾ cup whole fresh
cranberries
1 (1-liter) bottle club
soda, chilled
Garnish: fresh
cranberries, lime
slices

In a medium saucepan, combine sugar and water over medium heat. Stir in rosemary. Heat until sugar dissolves, stirring frequently. Add cranberries; cook until almost all cranberry skins pop, about 6 to 8 minutes, stirring occasionally. Cool; strain, discarding solids. Cover and chill syrup. Spoon about 2 tablespoons cranberry syrup into glasses; add desired amount of club soda. Garnish with fresh cranberries and lime slices, if desired.

Christmas Roses

Prepare the floral foam by soaking it in water. Line the tureen with foil, and place the wet foam inside. Insert the stems of the greenery throughout the foam. Wrap the pinecones with the floral picks, and then insert into the foam. For a final touch add roses and stems of berries throughout.

Hosting Guests

THE SPIRIT OF CHRISTMAS ABOUNDS
WITH FRIENDS AND FAMILY CAROLING OR
COMING OVER FOR BRUNCH OR FOR A
LIGHT DINNER TO EXCHANGE GIFTS. YOU
CAN CREATE YOUR OWN MENUS USING THIS
ASSORTMENT OF DELICIOUS RECIPES.

Peppermint-Mocha Brownies

MAKES 8 SERVINGS

1 (18.75-ounce) box
    brownie mix*
2 teaspoons instant
    coffee granules
1½ teaspoons
    peppermint extract
8 small peppermint
    candy canes
1 tablespoon
    confectioners' sugar

*We used Ghirardelli Chocolate
Supreme Brownie Mix.

Preheat oven to 325°. Line an 8-inch square baking pan with aluminum foil, allowing edges of foil to extend 2 inches over sides of pan. Spray foil with nonstick cooking spray.

Prepare brownie mix according to package directions, adding coffee granules and peppermint extract to batter. Spoon batter into prepared pan. Bake according to package directions. While brownie is still warm, top with candy canes, lightly pressing into warm brownie. Let cool completely in pan on a wire rack. Lift brownie from pan, using edges of foil as handles. Cut between candy canes into 8 brownies. Sift confectioners' sugar over brownies.

*I am always looking for new ways to wrap my gifts.
One year I wrapped every package in the same color,
and the results were stunning. I put a twist on it by using
no name tags and a different color bow for each person.
I was the only one who knew the "code," thereby avoiding
shaking and squeezing of presents. What fun!*

–PHYLLIS HOFFMAN DEPIANO

Peppermint Swirl Cupcakes

Preheat oven to 350°. Line 18 standard muffin pans and 18 mini muffin pans with paper liners; set aside. Prepare cake mix according to package directions, adding peppermints to batter. Bake mini cupcakes for 10 minutes, or until lightly browned. Bake standard cupcakes for 18 minutes, or until lightly browned. Let cool in pans for 5 minutes. Remove from pans, and let cool completely on a wire rack.

In a medium bowl, combine frosting and peppermint extract; stir well. Insert desired piping tip into a pastry bag. Using a small, clean paintbrush, paint 3 thin stripes of red food coloring inside pastry bag. Add frosting to prepared bag; pipe frosting onto cupcakes. Sprinkle with sanding sugar.

MAKES 18 STANDARD CUPCAKES AND 18 MINI CUPCAKES

1 (18.25-ounce) box white cake mix*
¼ cup finely ground peppermints
2 (16-ounce) containers white frosting
2 teaspoons peppermint extract
Red food coloring†
White sanding sugar

*We used Pillsbury Moist Supreme Classic White Cake Mix.

†We used Wilton Red-Red Icing Color.

*Christmas, my child, is love in action.
Every time we love, every time we give, it's Christmas.*

– DALE EVANS

Peppermint Chocolate Mousse

1 cup milk-chocolate
  morsels
¼ cup whipping cream
2 tablespoons water
2 teaspoons vanilla
  extract
1½ cups whipping
  cream, whipped

TOPPING
1 (8-ounce) package
  cream cheese,
  softened
½ cup sugar
1 (8-ounce) container
  vanilla yogurt
1 (8-ounce) container
  frozen nondairy
  whipped topping,
  thawed
12 peppermint candies,
  crushed

In a heavy saucepan, combine chocolate morsels, cream, and water; cook over low heat, stirring constantly, until chocolate melts. Cool. Stir in vanilla, and gently fold in whipped cream.

TOPPING In a medium bowl, beat cream cheese and sugar at medium speed with an electric mixer until smooth. Beat in yogurt until well blended. Stir in whipped topping just until blended.

In a glass mug, spoon mousse. Add topping. Sprinkle with crushed candies. Cover and refrigerate at least 1 hour or up to two days. Let stand 15 minutes before serving.

Peppermint Martini

Crush peppermint candies in a food processor. Dip rim of glass in corn syrup then in crushed peppermints. In a martini shaker, combine 1 cup white chocolate liqueur, 1/2 cup schnapps, 1/2 cup vodka, and ice. Shake, and strain into martini glasses. Repeat twice with remaining ingredients. Serve immediately.

MAKES 10 DRINKS

**Garnish: corn syrup,
    crushed peppermint**
**3 cups white chocolate
    liqueur**
**1½ cups peppermint
    schnapps**
1½ cups vodka

For somehow, not only at Christmas, but all the long year through, the joy that you give to others is the joy that comes back to you.

–JOHN GREENLEAF WHITTIER

Peppermint-Candy-Coated Pretzel Rods

Makes about 27 servings

8 ounces vanilla-flavored
candy coating
8 ounces chocolate-
flavored candy
coating
¼ teaspoon peppermint
candy flavoring,*
divided
1 (10-ounce) bag pretzel
rods†
½ cup crushed
peppermints

*We used Wilton Peppermint
Candy Flavoring.

†We used Snyder's of
Hanover Pretzel Rods.

Spray a wire rack with nonstick cooking spray. Cover a work surface with a sheet of wax paper; top with prepared wire rack. In a small bowl, melt vanilla candy coating according to package directions. Repeat with chocolate candy coating. Stir ⅛ teaspoon candy flavoring into each bowl of melted candy coating. Drizzle, dip, or spread candy coating over pretzel rods. While coated pretzel is still damp, sprinkle with crushed peppermints. Place on prepared wire rack. Let stand until firm, about 30 minutes. Gently remove from wire rack. Break off any large pieces of hardened candy coating, if desired.

Food should be fun.

– THOMAS KELLER

Cranberry-Walnut Blondies

Preheat oven to 350°. Spray a 13x9-inch baking pan with nonstick baking spray with flour.

In a large bowl, beat butter, brown sugar, and sugar until fluffy. Add eggs, one at a time, beating well after each addition. Add vanilla, beating well.

In a large bowl, sift together flour, salt, and baking soda. Gradually add flour mixture to butter mixture, beating well after each addition. Stir in cranberries, walnuts, and orange zest. Spoon batter into prepared pan. Bake for 30 minutes, or until a wooden pick inserted in the center of the blondies comes out clean. Cool completely in pan on a wire rack. Cut into triangles. Garnish with confectioners' sugar, if desired.

MAKES 32 PIECES

1 cup unsalted butter, melted
1 cup firmly packed light brown sugar
1 cup sugar
2 large eggs
2 teaspoons vanilla extract
2½ cups all-purpose flour
½ teaspoon salt
½ teaspoon baking soda
1 cup sweetened dried cranberries
½ cup chopped toasted walnuts
1 tablespoon orange zest
Garnish: ½ cup confectioners' sugar

A good conscience is a continual Christmas.

–BENJAMIN FRANKLIN

Double Chocolate Brownies

1 cup butter, softened
1 cup sugar
1 cup firmly packed light
    brown sugar
4 large eggs
1 teaspoon vanilla
    extract
1 cup all-purpose flour
½ cup unsweetened
    cocoa powder
½ teaspoon baking
    powder
½ teaspoon salt
1 cup semisweet
    chocolate morsels,
    melted and cooled
Garnish: cookie icing,
    Christmas confetti

Preheat oven to 350°. Spray a 13x9-inch baking pan with nonstick baking spray with flour.

In a large bowl, beat butter at medium-high speed with an electric mixer until fluffy. Add sugar and brown sugar to butter. Beat at medium speed with an electric mixer until fluffy. Add eggs, one at a time, beating well after each addition. Add vanilla, beating well.

In a medium bowl, sift together flour, cocoa powder, baking powder, and salt. Gradually add flour mixture to butter mixture, beating until smooth. Stir in cooled chocolate. Spread batter evenly into prepared pan. Bake for 25 to 30 minutes, or until a wooden pick inserted in the center of the brownies comes out clean. Cool completely in pan on a wire rack. Using a 3-inch cutter, cut into desired shapes. Garnish with cookie icing and Christmas confetti, if desired.

On Christmas morning, before we could open our Christmas presents, we would go to this stranger's home and bring them presents. I remember helping clean the house up and putting up a tree. My father believed that you have a responsibility to look after everyone else.

–GEORGE CLOONEY

White Christmas Chili

In a Dutch oven, heat 2 tablespoons olive oil over medium-high heat. Add chicken, chile pepper, cumin, salt, and coriander; add red pepper, if desired. Cook, stirring constantly, for 8 to 10 minutes or until browned. Remove chicken to a bowl.

In same pan, heat remaining 2 tablespoons olive oil over medium heat. Add onion, jalapeño peppers, garlic, and bay leaves. Cook for 4 to 5 minutes, stirring frequently, until tender. Add reserved chicken, chicken broth, and green chiles. Bring to a boil; reduce heat to a simmer, and cook, uncovered, for 15 minutes, stirring occasionally. Add beans; cook for 45 minutes, stirring occasionally. Remove and discard bay leaves. Add cheese and sour cream, stirring just until cheese is melted. Garnish with grated cheese, sour cream, ground red pepper, and cilantro, if desired.

MAKES 12 SERVINGS

- 4 tablespoons olive oil, divided
- 3 pounds boneless, skinless chicken breasts, cut into ½-inch pieces
- 1 tablespoon ground ancho chile pepper
- 2½ teaspoons ground cumin
- 1¼ teaspoons salt
- 1 teaspoon ground coriander
- ¼ teaspoon ground red pepper
- 2 cups chopped yellow onion
- 2 jalapeño peppers, seeded and minced
- 2 tablespoons minced garlic
- 4 bay leaves
- 1 quart chicken broth
- 2 (4-ounce) cans diced green chiles
- 2 (19-ounce) cans cannellini beans, drained
- 2 (15.5-ounce) cans great Northern beans, drained
- 4 cups grated Monterey Jack cheese
- 1 cup sour cream
- Garnish: grated cheese, sour cream, ground red pepper, cilantro

Marinated Shrimp

1 (2-pound) bag
    frozen shrimp,
    peeled, deveined,
    and tails on, thawed
2 small red onions,
    sliced
2 large lemons, sliced
3 limes, sliced
1 cup olive oil
1 cup red wine vinegar
3 tablespoons sugar
1 tablespoon lemon zest
1 tablespoon lime zest
½ teaspoon salt

In a large glass trifle bowl, layer shrimp, onion slices, lemon slices, and lime slices; repeat layers, if needed.

In a small bowl, whisk together oil, vinegar, sugar, lemon zest, lime zest, and salt; pour over shrimp. Cover, and chill overnight.

Bright White

Arrange fresh magnolia leaves and green hypericum berries to showcase the beauty and texture of large white hydrangeas.

Cheese Grits Cakes with Smoked Sausage and Sweet Pepper Relish

Lightly grease an 11x7-inch baking dish. In a medium saucepan, bring cream, broth, and salt to a boil over medium-high heat. Whisk in grits. Cover, reduce heat, and simmer for 5 minutes or until thickened. Add cheese, stirring until melted.

Spread grits into prepared dish. Cover, and refrigerate for 8 hours, or until set.

In a large skillet, brown sausage, in batches, on both sides over medium-high heat; remove from skillet, and let cool.

Preheat oven to broil. To serve, slice grits into 42 squares. Top each with a sausage slice. Place on a broiler pan. Broil for 3 to 4 minutes; top each with 1 teaspoon relish.

MAKES 42 SQUARES

2 cups whipping cream
3 cups chicken broth
1 teaspoon salt
1½ cups quick cooking grits
1 cup shredded sharp Cheddar cheese
1 (16-ounce) package smoked sausage, sliced into 42 slices (½ inch thick)
1 (11-ounce) jar sweet pepper relish

Setting the table with holiday china sets a festive mood for a meal in a beautiful, subtle way. Formal or informal patterns can be accented with solid accent plates and accessorized with complimentary napkins and napkin rings.

–PHYLLIS HOFFMAN DEPIANO

Roasted Pork Tenderloin Sandwiches with Cranberry-Orange Sauce

MAKES 20 SANDWICHES

**2 (³/4-pound) pork
 tenderloins**
¼ cup soy sauce
¼ cup olive oil
**1 teaspoon minced fresh
 ginger**
1 teaspoon sesame oil
¼ teaspoon hot sauce
2 cloves garlic, crushed
**3 dozen store-bought
 party rolls, warmed**
**Cranberry-Orange Sauce
 (recipe follows)**

**CRANBERRY-ORANGE
SAUCE**
MAKES 1½ CUPS

**1 (16-ounce) can
 whole-berry
 cranberry sauce**
¼ cup fresh orange juice
1 tablespoon orange zest
½ teaspoon salt
**¼ teaspoon ground
 black pepper**

In a zip-top plastic bag, add tenderloins. Set aside.

In a small bowl, combine soy sauce and next five ingredients. Pour mixture into bag; seal. Marinate in the refrigerator for 3 hours, turning bag occasionally.

Preheat oven to 450°. In a roasting pan, add tenderloins. Bake for 15 minutes; reduce oven temperature to 350°, and bake for 15 to 20 minutes or until a meat thermometer inserted into thickest portion reads 140°, or the desired degree of doneness is reached.

Let pork stand for 20 minutes; slice into 20 slices. Serve on rolls with Cranberry-Orange Sauce.

CRANBERRY-ORANGE SAUCE In a small bowl, combine cranberry sauce, orange juice, orange zest, salt, and pepper. Chill, if desired.

Shortbread Cookies

Preheat oven to 350°.

In a large bowl, beat butter and sugar at medium speed with an electric mixer until combined. Add vanilla. Slowly add flour, beating at low speed until dough comes together. Place on a lightly floured surface, and shape into a flat disk. Wrap in plastic, and chill for 30 minutes.

On lightly floured surface, roll dough to a $1/2$-inch thickness, and cut with a $2^1/2$-inch round fluted cutter. Place cookies on an ungreased baking sheet, and sprinkle with sugar.

Bake for 20 to 25 minutes or until edges begin to brown. Let cool on pan for 10 minutes. Remove from pan, and cool completely on a wire rack.

MAKES 20 COOKIES

1½ cups butter, softened
1 cup sugar
1 teaspoon vanilla extract
3½ cups all-purpose flour
Sugar for dusting

The cookie jar is never quite as full as at Christmas. I love using all of my favorite spices like cinnamon and nutmeg, and my big cookie sheets and plethora of cookie cutters.

–PHYLLIS HOFFMAN DEPIANO

White Chocolate Fudge

2 cups sugar
½ teaspoon salt
6 tablespoons butter
1 cup whipping cream
3½ cups mini
marshmallows
3 cups white chocolate
morsels, coarsely
chopped
1 teaspoon vanilla
extract
½ cup crushed
peppermints or
chopped pistachios

Line a 13x9-inch baking pan with 2 strips of wax paper (one lengthwise, one crosswise) so ends hang over sides of pan; coat evenly with nonstick cooking spray. Set aside.

In a large heavy saucepan, combine sugar, salt, butter, cream, and marshmallows over medium heat, stirring about 5 to 6 minutes or until butter and marshmallows are almost melted.

Bring mixture to a boil over medium-high heat; cook, stirring occasionally, for 5 minutes. Remove from heat. Add chopped morsels and vanilla; stir until melted. Pour mixture into prepared pan.

Let fudge cool in pan at room temperature for 3 hours. Use edges of wax paper to lift out fudge; place on a cutting board, and remove wax paper. Cut into 24 squares; top with crushed peppermints or chopped pistachios.

I have a silver bell collection and love adding one to it every year. They sit proudly near the tree and reflect the tiny tree lights beautifully!

–PHYLLIS HOFFMAN DEPIANO

Orange Squares

Preheat oven to 350°.

In a bowl, beat butter and 1/2 cup sugar at medium speed with an electric mixer until creamy; reduce speed to low, and add 2 cups flour, beating until blended. On a well-floured surface, roll dough into a ball. Place dough in a 13x9-inch baking pan; press dough up sides of pan. Chill.

Bake crust for 15 to 20 minutes, or until very lightly browned. Let cool on a wire rack.

For the filling, in a large bowl, whisk together eggs, 3 cups sugar, zest, juice, and flour. Pour over crust, and bake for 30 to 35 minutes or until filling is set.

1 cup butter, softened
1/2 cup sugar
2 cups all-purpose flour
6 extra-large eggs
3 cups sugar
2 tablespoons orange zest
1 cup freshly squeezed orange juice
1 cup all-purpose flour
Confectioners' sugar

"Glory to God in the highest...and on earth peace among men with whom He is pleased."

–LUKE 2:14 NASB

Pecan Pie Bars with Chocolate

MAKES 20 LARGE SQUARES

2½ cups butter,
    softened
¾ cup sugar
3 extra-large eggs
1 teaspoon vanilla
    extract
4½ cups flour
½ teaspoon baking
    powder
2 cups butter
1 cup honey
3 cups firmly packed
    light brown sugar
2 teaspoons lemon zest
¼ cup whipping cream
2 pounds pecans,
    coarsely chopped
1 cup chocolate morsels

Preheat oven to 350°.

For the crust, in a large bowl, beat butter and ¾ cup sugar at medium speed with a mixer until fluffy, about 3 minutes. Add eggs and vanilla, beating until blended. In a bowl, combine flour and baking powder. Add to butter mixture, beating at low speed until combined.

Pat dough evenly into an ungreased 18x12-inch baking sheet, pressing up sides of pan. (Dough will be sticky. Sprinkle hands with flour to press dough into pan.) Bake for 15 minutes, or until crust is set but not browned. Let cool. For the topping, in a large heavy saucepan, combine butter, honey, brown sugar, and zest. Cook over low heat until butter is melted, stirring constantly with a wooden spoon. Bring mixture to a boil over medium-high heat, and cook for 3 minutes. Remove from heat. Stir in cream and pecans.

Pour over crust, trying not to get the filling between the crust and pan.

Bake for 25 to 30 minutes, or until filling is set. Remove from oven, and cool completely on a wire rack. Place chocolate morsels in zip-top bag. Microwave for 30 seconds. Mush chocolate around in hands until smooth. Snip corner with sissors. Drizzle over bars. Wrap in plastic wrap and refrigerate until chilled. Cut into bars, and serve.

Champagne Punch

Combine cranberry juice, orange juice, lemon juice, and sugar, stir well; chill for at least 8 hours.

Pour juice mixture into punch bowl. Garnish with orange slices if desired. Gently stir in chilled Champagne just before serving.

2 cups cranberry juice cocktail
½ cup orange juice
1 cup lemon juice
½ cup sugar
3 bottles (750-milliliter) Champagne, chilled
Garnish: orange slices

Note: Nonalcoholic sparkling grape juice can be substituted for Champagne.

Arrange food around the perimeter of tables to allow guests easy access. Create varying heights with serving pieces to show off your selections.

–PHYLLIS HOFFMAN DEPIANO

Cherry Pineapple Cheer

2 cups pineapple juice
¼ cup maraschino
cherry syrup
8 maraschino cherries
1 (750-milliliter) bottle
Prosecco

In a medium bowl, combine pineapple juice and cherry syrup.

Place 1 cherry in the bottom of each Champagne flute. Pour ¼ cup pineapple mixture into bottom of each flute. Top with Prosecco.

Special Touches

Classic patterned papers and metallic ribbons add to the sparkle under the tree. Add the finishing touch with petite cards and gift tags.

Caramel Dessert Cups

In each dessert cup, spoon 1 tablespoon *dulce de leche*. Top with fruit and whipped cream.

Garnish with fresh mint, if desired. Serve immediately.

Makes 6 servings

6 purchased dessert cups
6 tablespoons *dulce de leche*
1 cup fresh raspberries
1 cup fresh blueberries
3 large strawberries, halved
Sweetened whipped cream or frozen whipped topping, thawed
Garnish: fresh mint

Magnolia leaves, berries, and boxwood cuttings are wonderful gifts from outdoors. You can mix with red blooms to complete your holiday décor.

–PHYLLIS HOFFMAN DEPIANO

Vegetable Pinwheels

1 tablespoon vegetable oil
½ pound zucchini, diced
¼ cup chopped roasted
   red bell pepper
2 cloves garlic, minced
1 teaspoon coarse
   kosher salt
1 teaspoon freshly
   ground black pepper
2 tablespoons prepared
   pesto
2 tablespoons prepared
   garlic hummus
1 (8-ounce) can
   refrigerated crescent
   rolls

Preheat oven to 350°. Line 2 rimmed baking sheets with parchment paper. In a medium skillet, heat oil over medium-high heat. Add zucchini, and cook for 4 minutes, stirring frequently, or until zucchini starts to brown. Add bell pepper, garlic, salt, and pepper; cook for 2 minutes, stirring frequently. Spoon zucchini mixture into a bowl; let cool for 10 minutes. Cover and refrigerate for 30 minutes.

In a small bowl, combine pesto and garlic hummus. Divide crescent roll dough into 4 equal rectangles, pressing seams together to seal. Spread pesto mixture over each dough rectangle in a thin, even layer. Spread cooled zucchini mixture over each prepared dough rectangle.

Starting with long side, roll up dough, jelly-roll style, and place seam side down on parchment paper. Slice each rectangle into 1-inch slices.

Place on prepared pans 2 inches apart. Bake for 15 to 18 minutes or until edges of pastry are golden brown. Serve immediately.

I will honor Christmas in my heart,
and try to keep it all the year.

–CHARLES DICKENS

Crab Cake Stuffed Shrimp

Line a rimmed baking sheet with parchment paper. In a medium skillet, heat 5 tablespoons butter over medium heat until melted. Add onion, and cook, stirring frequently, for about 8 minutes or until onion is tender. Add bell peppers, remaining 5 tablespoons butter, white wine, and garlic, stirring to combine well. Cook for 4 minutes, or until bell peppers are tender. In a large bowl, add crabmeat, onion mixture, cracker crumbs, panko, red pepper, Old Bay, salt, and black pepper, stirring to combine well. Cover and refrigerate for at least 1 hour, or up to 24 hours.

Preheat oven to 350°. Using a sharp knife and starting at the tail end, butterfly each shrimp, cutting to, but not through, underside of shrimp; remove and discard vein. On a clean flat surface, place each shrimp butterflied side down, pressing to flatten. Form about 3 tablespoons crab mixture into an oval. Place on top of shrimp, pressing the shrimp tail over the crab mixture to secure. Repeat with remaining shrimp and crab mixture. Place shrimp on prepared pan. Bake for about 8 minutes, or until a meat thermometer inserted into center of shrimp tails reaches 145°. Serve immediately.

MAKES 2 DOZEN

10 tablespoons unsalted butter, divided
1 cup chopped yellow onion
1 cup chopped green bell pepper
1 cup chopped red bell pepper
½ cup dry white wine
2 cloves garlic, minced
2 (8-ounce) containers jumbo lump crabmeat, picked free of shell
1 sleeve round buttery crackers (about 30 crackers), crushed
½ cup panko (Japanese bread crumbs)
½ teaspoon ground red pepper
1 teaspoon Old Bay Seasoning
1 teaspoon kosher salt
1 teaspoon ground black pepper
24 large fresh shrimp, peeled (tails left on)

Frenchie Turkey Sliders

1 (1-pound) package
   applewood-or
   cider-smoked bacon
2 pounds ground turkey
   breast
1 tablespoon chopped
   fresh parsley
2 teaspoons coarse
   kosher salt
2 teaspoons freshly
   ground black pepper
½ teaspoon ground
   cumin
½ teaspoon paprika
1 (8-ounce) Brie round
2 medium Granny Smith
   apples
12 slider buns

Preheat oven to 350°. Line 2 rimmed baking sheets with heavy-duty aluminum foil. Place a wire rack on top of each baking sheet. Place bacon on tops of racks in an even layer. Bake for 18 to 20 minutes or until crisp; set aside. In a large bowl, combine turkey, parsley, salt, pepper, cumin, and paprika, mixing to combine. Divide turkey mixture into 12 equal portions. Preheat a grill pan over medium-high heat. Grill turkey patties for about 6 minutes on each side or until a meat thermometer inserted into center of patty registers 155°. Remove rind from Brie, and slice into 12 equal slices. Slice apples in half crosswise, and remove cores. Slice apple halves crosswise into ¼-inch-thick slices. Top bottoms of slider buns with turkey patties, Brie, bacon, and apple slices. Secure with a sandwich pick, if desired. Serve immediately.

An ornament party is a fun way to swap gifts without buying individual ones. It is the sharing of conversation and special little holiday foods that is memorable.

–PHYLLIS HOFFMAN DEPIANO

Chewy Gingerbread Cookies with Orange Glaze

Preheat oven to 350°. Line baking sheets with parchment paper. In a medium bowl, whisk together flour, cinnamon, ginger, allspice, baking soda, salt, cloves, baking powder, cardamom, and red pepper. In a large bowl, combine butter, brown sugar, orange zest, and orange extract. Beat at medium speed with a mixer until creamy. Add egg, beating to combine. Beat in molasses and honey, scraping down sides of bowl as necessary. Gradually add flour mixture, beating until well combined. On a lightly floured surface, roll dough to $1/3$-inch thickness. Using desired cookie cutters, cut out dough, and place on prepared baking sheets, rerolling dough as needed. Bake for 10 to 14 minutes, rotating halfway through baking, until edges are lightly browned. Let cool on pans for 2 minutes. Remove from pans, and let cool completely on wire racks. Dip top sides of cookies into glaze, and place on parchment paper, glazed side up. Let stand for 30 minutes, or until set. Repeat procedure, if desired. Garnish with cinnamon sugar, if desired.

ORANGE GLAZE
Makes 3 cups

3 to 4 cups confectioners' sugar, sifted
$1/4$ cup orange juice
1 teaspoon orange extract

In a medium bowl, combine 3 cups confectioners' sugar, orange juice, and orange extract, whisking until smooth. Add more sugar to reach desired consistency.

Tip: The thinner the glaze, the more it will harden on cookie.

Makes 1 dozen (6-inch) cookies

3 cups all-purpose flour
2 teaspoons ground cinnamon
$1\frac{1}{2}$ teaspoons ground ginger
$1/2$ teaspoon ground allspice
$1/2$ teaspoon baking soda
$1/2$ teaspoon coarse kosher salt
$1/4$ teaspoon ground cloves
$1/4$ teaspoon baking powder
$1/4$ teaspoon ground cardamom
$1/8$ teaspoon ground red pepper
$1/2$ cup unsalted butter, softened
$1/2$ cup firmly packed dark brown sugar
1 tablespoon orange zest
1 teaspoon orange extract
1 large egg
$1/4$ cup blackstrap molasses
$1/2$ cup honey
Orange Glaze (recipe follows)
Garnish: cinnamon sugar

Red Velvet Cupcakes

MAKES 2 DOZEN

1½ cups all-purpose flour
1½ cups cake flour
½ cup unsweetened
    cocoa powder
1½ teaspoons baking soda
1 teaspoon plus
    ⅛ teaspoon coarse
    kosher salt, divided
2 cups butter, melted
    and cooled, divided
2 cups sugar
4 large eggs
1½ cups whole buttermilk
1 cup vegetable oil
1 tablespoon white
    vinegar
2 tablespoons plus 2
    teaspoons vanilla
    extract, divided
1 tablespoon liquid red
    food coloring
2 (8-ounce) packages
    cream cheese,
    room temperature
6 to 7 cups confectioners'
    sugar
Garnish: crushed hard
    peppermint candies,
    crushed soft
    peppermint candies

Preheat oven to 350°. Line 2 (12-cup) muffin pans with cupcake liners. In a medium bowl, whisk together flours, cocoa, baking soda, and 1 teaspoon salt. In a large bowl, beat 1 cup melted butter and sugar at medium speed with a mixer until fluffy. Add eggs, one at a time, beating well after each addition. Add buttermilk, oil, vinegar, and 2 teaspoons vanilla. Gradually add flour mixture to butter mixture, beating to combine well. Add red food coloring. Evenly divide batter among muffin cups, filling about two-thirds full. Bake for 18 to 22 minutes or until a wooden pick inserted in centers comes out clean, rotating halfway through baking. Let cool in pans for 5 minutes. Remove from pans, and let cool completely on wire racks.

In a large bowl, combine cream cheese, remaining 1 cup melted butter, remaining 2 tablespoons vanilla, and remaining ⅛ teaspoon salt. Beat at medium speed with a mixer until creamy. Reduce mixer speed to medium-low, and gradually add confectioners' sugar, 2 cups at a time, until desired spreading consistency is reached. Frost tops of cupcakes. Garnish with crushed peppermint, if desired.

Cranberry Cocktail

In a large pitcher, combine Prosecco, cranberry juice, lemon juice, and cranberries, stirring well. Serve immediately.

Makes approximately
8 servings

**1 (750-milliliter) bottle
Prosecco, chilled
4 cups cranberry juice
cocktail, chilled
2 tablespoons fresh
lemon juice
½ cup fresh cranberries**

*Before my guests arrive,
I view the serving areas
from different angles to be
sure every view is attractive.*

-PHYLLIS HOFFMAN DEPIANO

Avocado Dip

MAKES APPROXIMATELY
8 TO 10 SERVINGS

4 large avocados,
   peeled, pitted, and
   chopped
½ cup halved grape
   tomatoes
½ cup canned black
   beans, rinsed and
   drained
¼ cup chopped red onion
3 tablespoons chopped
   fresh cilantro
2 tablespoons lime juice
2 tablespoons
   extra-virgin olive oil
½ teaspoon garlic salt
Tortilla chips

In a large bowl, combine avocados, tomatoes, beans, red onion, cilantro, lime juice, olive oil, and garlic salt, tossing gently to combine. Serve immediately with tortilla chips.

I like to have a big lovely amaryllis bulb blooming by Christmas day. Pink, red, white, salmon, orange, and striped, originally from South America, they are loved the world over.

–PHYLLIS HOFFMAN DEPIANO

Chicken Skewers & Sauce

Skewer 3 pieces popcorn chicken alternately with 1 pineapple wedge and 1 bell pepper square onto each skewer.

In a medium bowl, combine chili garlic sauce, brown sugar, vinegar, and Worcestershire, whisking well. In the bottom of each serving glass, place 2 tablespoons sauce. Place 2 prepared skewers in each glass. Serve immediately.

MAKES 8 SERVINGS

16 (4-inch) skewers
48 pieces popcorn chicken,* cooked according to package directions
12 (1-inch) wedges fresh pineapple
12 (1-inch) squares green bell pepper
3/4 cup Asian chili garlic sauce
1/4 cup plus 2 tablespoons firmly packed light brown sugar
2 tablespoons apple cider vinegar
1 tablespoon Worcestershire sauce

*We used Tyson Any'tizers Popcorn Chicken.

Mini Pizzas

MAKES 16 PIZZAS

1½ cups shredded Italian
   6-cheese blend
½ cup shredded mild
   Cheddar cheese
¼ cup chopped green
   onion
¼ cup finely chopped
   red bell pepper
⅓ cup mayonnaise
16 mini pitas
48 mini pepperoni slices
4 queen-size stuffed
   Spanish olives, sliced
   into fourths

Preheat oven to 400°. Line a baking sheet with parchment paper.

In a medium bowl, combine 6-cheese blend, Cheddar cheese, green onion, red bell pepper, and mayonnaise, mixing well. Divide evenly among pitas. Place 3 mini pepperoni slices and 1 olive slice on each pizza. Bake for 6 to 8 minutes, or until cheese is melted and lightly golden. Serve immediately.

Elves' Time Off Playlist

"Little Saint Nick" — The Beach Boys   "Santa Claus Is Coming to Town" — Frank Sinatra

"Santa Baby" — Eartha Kitt   "Rudolph the Red-Nosed Reindeer" — Jack Johnson

"I'm Gonna Lasso Santa Claus" — Brenda Lee   "Here Comes Santa Claus" — Bing Crosby

"Santa Bring My Baby Back to Me" — Elvis Presley   "Run, Rudolph, Run" — Chuck Berry

"Boogie Woogie Santa Claus" — Mabel Scott   "Up on the Housetop" — Jimmy Buffett

"We Are Santa's Elves" — The Silver and Gold Singers

"¿Dónde Está Santa Claus?" — Augie Rios

"I Saw Mommy Kissing Santa Claus" — The Jackson 5

Cheesecake

Raspberry
sauce

Chocolate
sauce

Caramel
sauce

Cheesecake with Raspberry Sauce

CHEESECAKE To make your party prep easier, purchase a frozen cheesecake from your grocery store. Then, all you need for a fabulous dessert are sauces and toppings. We served purchased chocolate and caramel sauces and included a homemade raspberry sauce (see recipe) as well. For toppings, fill bowls with favorite candies that you've chopped or crushed.

RASPBERRY SAUCE In a large saucepan, combine raspberries, sugar, and Chambord, stirring well. Bring to a simmer over medium heat, stirring often. Simmer for 10 minutes or until sauce is thickened, stirring often. Cool completely. (Sauce may be made up to 2 days ahead and stored, tightly covered, in the refrigerator.)

MAKES 3 CUPS

24 ounces frozen raspberries
½ cup sugar
½ cup Chambord

Make the most of your holiday dinner party by turning it into a perfect occasion to give to those in need. Have guests bring toys to donate to a local charity.

Christmas Veggie Tree

1 **(24-inch-high x 9-inch-diameter) urethane cone form**
3 **heads curly leaf lettuce, washed and dried**
Wooden picks
5 **pints cherry tomatoes, washed and dried**
10 **whole button mushrooms, stems removed and cut into stars**
2 **yellow bell peppers, seeded and cut into rings**
1 **red bell pepper, seeded and cut into candy-cane shape**
2 **cups radishes, washed and trimmed***
4 **cups fresh broccoli florets**
1 **(8-ounce) block mozzarella cheese**
1 **(8-ounce) block sharp Cheddar cheese**
1 **(15-ounce) can whole black olives, drained**
1 **(5x1/2-inch-thick) provolone slice**

Use a channel knife to cut designs in radishes, if desired.

Starting at bottom, cover the form with lettuce, allowing 1 inch of bottom of lettuce leaf to overlap with top of lettuce leaf below it.

Arrange tomatoes around the form in the shape of a garland, securing each with a wooden pick. Place mushrooms, yellow bell peppers, red bell peppers, radishes, and broccoli on the tree as desired, securing with wooden picks.

Cut block of mozzarella in half horizontally. Using 1- to 1 1/2-inch star- or snowflake-shaped cutters, cut desired shapes out of mozzarella. Repeat procedure with Cheddar cheese. Place cheese shapes on tree, securing with wooden picks.

Using a (4-inch) star-shaped cutter, cut out a star from provolone cheese slice. Place a wooden pick in the top of tree. Place cheese star on pick. Serve with your favorite dip.

Handmade Gifts

HANDMADE GIFTS OF LOVE WILL PLEASE
ANYONE ON YOUR LIST—INCLUDING SANTA.
CLEVER IDEAS AND RECIPES ALL WRAPPED IN
FUN MAKE GIVING MORE FUN THAN RECEIVING.

Christmas Fudge

2/3 cup whole milk

3/4 cup butter

2 cups sugar

3 (4-ounce) white
chocolate bars,
chopped

1 (7-ounce) jar
marshmallow crème

3/4 cup chopped roasted
pistachios

3/4 cup finely chopped
dried cherries

Line a 13x9-inch baking pan with aluminum foil, allowing foil to extend over sides of pan. In a medium saucepan, combine milk, butter, and sugar over high heat, whisking often. Bring mixture to a rolling boil. Reduce heat to medium, stirring constantly, until mixture reaches 234° on a candy thermometer. Remove from heat; add chocolate, marshmallow crème, nuts, and cherries, stirring until smooth. Spread into prepared pan. Chill for 4 hours, or until set. Cut into squares to serve.

Perfect Place Cards

For simple sweet place cards, use decorated gingerbread boy cookies. Write guests' names across the frosted cookies and tie tiny ribbons around the necks to resemble scarves.

Gingerbread Snack Mix

Preheat oven to 325°. Line a rimmed baking sheet with foil.

In a medium bowl, combine melted butter, brown sugar, and cinnamon. Add all nuts, tossing gently to coat. Spread nuts in a single layer on prepared pan. Bake for 16 minutes, stirring halfway through baking time. Let cool completely.

In a large bowl, combine cookies, cereal, cranberries, and raisins. Stir in nut mixture and white chocolate morsels. Store in an airtight container for up to 5 days.

Note: Gingerbread cookie rounds were cut from dough scraps using a 1-inch cutter.

MAKES 10 CUPS

¼ **cup butter, melted**
¼ **cup firmly packed brown sugar**
1 **teaspoon ground cinnamon**
1 **cup macadamia nuts**
1 **cup pecan halves**
1 **cup walnut halves**
2 **cups 1-inch gingerbread cookie rounds**
2 **cups crispy corn-and-rice cereal***
1 **cup dried cranberries**
1 **cup golden raisins**
1 **cup white chocolate morsels**

*We used Crispix.

Hand-wrapped gifts are the best—lots of curly ribbons and beautiful papers. You can embellish with stickers, charms or small twigs or greenery fronds.

–PHYLLIS HOFFMAN DEPIANO

Festive Snack Mix

MAKES ABOUT 14 CUPS

2 (3.2-ounce) bags
    microwave
    butter-flavored
    popcorn
2 teaspoons ground
    mustard
1½ teaspoons ground
    coriander
1 teaspoon ground
    ginger
2 cups honey-roasted
    sesame sticks
2 cups wasabi peas
2 cups bagel chips

Prepare popcorn according to package directions. While popcorn is hot, sprinkle with mustard, coriander, and ginger. In a large bowl, toss together popcorn, sesame sticks, peas, and bagel chips. Store, covered, at room temperature for up to one week.

For the Musician
Make a photo copy of Christmas sheet music to wrap your gift. Tie with baker's twine threaded through small jingle bells, and form a bow on top of package.

Basic Gingerbread Cookies

In a large bowl, beat shortening and sugars with a mixer at medium speed until fluffy. Add egg, beating until combined. Add molasses, beating until smooth.

In a medium bowl, combine flour and next 4 ingredients. Gradually add to shortening mixture, beating until combined. Divide dough in half, and form each half into a disk. Wrap each in heavy-duty plastic wrap, and chill for at least one hour or up to 3 days.

Preheat oven to 350°. Line baking sheets with parchment paper.

On a lightly floured surface, roll dough to 1/4-inch thickness. Cut dough using desired cutters. Place 3 to 4 inches apart on prepared pans, and bake for 6 to 8 minutes. Edges of cookies should be lightly browned. Let cool on pans for 2 minutes. Remove from pans, and let cool completely on wire racks.

Decorate cookies with Meringue Frosting. Store in an airtight container for up to 1 week.

MERINGUE FROSTING In a small bowl, whisk 1/4 cup cold water and meringue powder until foamy. Gradually add confectioners' sugar, whisking until smooth. Divide mixture into small bowls, and tint with desired color of food coloring paste.

YIELD VARIES DEPENDING ON CUTTER SIZE

1 cup butter-flavored shortening
3/4 cup firmly packed brown sugar
1/4 cup granulated sugar
1 large egg
3/4 cup unsulfured molasses
5 cups all-purpose flour
2 teaspoons pumpkin pie spice
1 teaspoon baking soda
1/4 teaspoon salt
1/4 teaspoon ground cloves
Meringue Frosting (recipe follows)

MERINGUE FROSTING
MAKES ABOUT 1 1/2 CUPS

1/4 cup cold water
3 tablespoons meringue powder
2 cups confectioners' sugar
Food coloring paste, assorted colors

Gingerbread Man Cookie Sandwiches

Makes 6 sandwich
cookies

**Cookie Cream Filling
(recipe follows)
12 decorated 4½-inch
gingerbread man
cookies**

COOKIE CREAM FILLING
Makes 2 cups

**1 (8-ounce) container
frozen whipped
topping, thawed
½ (8-ounce) package
cream cheese,
softened
¼ cup confectioners'
sugar**

Spread or pipe about ⅓ cup Cookie Cream Filling on half of cookies. Top with remaining cookies. Serve immediately.

COOKIE CREAM FILLING In a medium bowl, beat whipped topping and cream cheese with a mixer at medium speed until smooth. Beat in confectioners' sugar. Cover, and chill for 1 hour. Let come to room temperature before filling cookies.

You can spread holiday cheer with homemade cookies and bars. I try and make cookies with my grandchildren before Christmas eve. They love rolling, cutting, and of course decorating-the icing part!

–PHYLLIS HOFFMAN DEPIANO

Peppermint Marshmallow Bars

Preheat oven to 350°. Line a 13x9-inch baking pan with parchment paper, allowing excess to hang over sides.

In a medium bowl, combine graham cracker crumbs, 1 cup granulated sugar, butter, and beaten egg white. Press mixture into bottom of prepared pan. Bake for 10 minutes or until set. Let cool completely. Chill for 30 minutes.

Meanwhile, in a small bowl, pour $3/4$ cup cold water. Sprinkle gelatin over water; let stand for 5 minutes to soften.

In a heavy-bottomed saucepan, combine remaining 3 cups granulated sugar, corn syrup, $3/4$ cup hot water, and salt. Cook, stirring constantly, over medium heat, until sugar dissolves. Continue cooking without stirring until a candy thermometer registers 240° (soft ball stage). Remove from heat; add gelatin mixture.

In the bowl of a stand mixer fitted with the whisk attachment, beat egg whites on high speed until stiff peaks form. With mixer running, slowly add gelatin mixture in a steady stream. Add extracts, and continue beating for 10 minutes or until stiff and glossy.

Spread marshmallow mixture over prepared crust. Drop food coloring onto surface of marshmallows. Using a sharp knife, swirl the food coloring into marshmallows to create swirls. Dust with confectioners' sugar, and chill for 8 hours or overnight. Using parchment, remove from pan. Cut into bars. Store at room temperature for up to 5 days.

MAKES 12 TO 16 SERVINGS

4 cups chocolate graham cracker crumbs
4 cups granulated sugar, divided
1 cup butter, melted
1 egg white, lightly beaten
$3/4$ cup cold water
$3\frac{1}{2}$ tablespoons unflavored gelatin
$3/4$ cup light corn syrup
$3/4$ cup hot water
$1/4$ teaspoon salt
3 egg whites
1 teaspoon vanilla extract
1 teaspoon peppermint extract
6 to 8 drops liquid red food coloring
Confectioners' sugar

Chocolate Chip Biscotti

MAKES ABOUT 2 DOZEN

2/3 cup sugar
2 large eggs
1 teaspoon vanilla extract
1¾ cups all-purpose flour
¼ cup unsweetened
    cocoa powder
¾ teaspoon baking
    powder
⅛ teaspoon salt
¾ cup chopped roasted
    and salted pistachios
½ cup miniature
    chocolate morsels

Preheat oven to 350°. Line a baking sheet with parchment paper.

In a medium bowl, beat sugar, eggs, and vanilla with a mixer at medium speed until thick and pale. In a small bowl, combine flour, cocoa, baking powder, and salt. Gradually add flour mixture to sugar mixture, beating until combined. Beat in pistachios and chocolate morsels. Shape dough into an 11x3½-inch log on prepared pan.

Bake for 20 minutes. Using a serrated knife, cut log crosswise into ½-inch-thick slices. Place slices cut side down on pan. Bake for 8 minutes. Turn slices over, and bake 8 minutes more.

Remove from pan, and let cool completely on a wire rack. Store in airtight containers for up to 1 week.

Cookie Tins

Gather old cookie tins from your stash of holiday decorations, or check out secondhand shops. Place a glass inside the tin, and fill it with water. Cut roses and hypericum berries to the desired length, and slip into the glass. For a nostalgic centerpiece, fill a variety of tins, and place them down the center of a table.

Cranberry-Pistachio Pretzel Bark

In a large microwave-safe bowl, microwave 3½ packages white chocolate morsels on HIGH in 30-second intervals, stirring between each, until melted and smooth (about 2½ minutes total). Stir in pretzels. Spread on parchment paper in an even layer.

Sprinkle with cranberries and pistachios, and gently press into chocolate mixture.

In a small microwave-safe bowl, microwave remaining ½ package white chocolate morsels on HIGH in 30-second intervals, stirring between each, until melted and smooth (about 1 minute total).

Using a piping bag or squeeze bottle, drizzle melted chocolate over cranberries and pistachios. Let cool for 2 hours or until completely set. Break into pieces. Store in airtight containers.

MAKES ABOUT 3 POUNDS

4 (11-ounce) packages white chocolate morsels, divided
3 cups crushed pretzels
1 cup dried cranberries
1 cup chopped pistachios

When I give gifts from the kitchen, I try to make them look as good as they taste.

–PHYLLIS HOFFMAN DEPIANO

Smokey Cheesy Bacon Loaves

MAKES 6 (6-INCH) LOAVES

1/4 cup butter
1 1/2 cups finely chopped
   sweet onion
6 cups all-purpose flour
2 tablespoons baking
   powder
1 teaspoon salt
2 cups shredded smoked
   white Cheddar cheese
1 cup shredded smoked
   Gouda cheese
2 cups whole milk
1 cup sour cream
1/2 cup butter, melted
2 large eggs, lightly
   beaten
10 slices bacon, cooked
   and crumbled

In a medium skillet, melt 1/4 cup butter over medium heat. Add onion, and cook for 8 to 10 minutes or until tender. Increase heat to medium-high, and cook, stirring constantly, for 4 to 5 minutes or until onion is lightly browned. Remove from heat, and let cool slightly.

Preheat oven to 350°. Spray 6 (6x3-inch) loaf pans with baking spray with flour.

In a large bowl, combine flour, baking powder, and salt. Add cheeses, stirring to combine.

In a medium bowl, combine milk, sour cream, 1/2 cup melted butter, and beaten eggs. Add to flour mixture, stirring until dry ingredients are combined. Stir in bacon and caramelized onions. Spoon batter into prepared pans, and bake for 30 to 35 minutes or until a wooden pick inserted in center comes out clean. Let cool in pans for 10 minutes. Remove from pans, and let cool completely on wire racks.

I put on my favorite Christmas carols to wrap my packages. I really enjoy wrapping for the small children with sparkles and bright prints. They can usually spot their gifts first under the tree!

–PHYLLIS HOFFMAN DEPIANO

Pecan-Topped Spice Cake Bites

Bake cake mix according to package directions. Let cool completely, and crumble into a bowl.

In a large bowl, beat cream cheese and butter with a mixer at medium speed until creamy. Add confectioners' sugar, beating until smooth. Beat in apple butter. Add crumbled cake to cream cheese mixture, and beat at medium speed until smooth. Cover and chill for 2 hours or up to 2 days.

Line a rimmed baking sheet with parchment paper. Roll cake mixture into 1½-inch balls, and place on prepared pan. Insert a lollipop stick into top of each cake ball. Cover and freeze for 2 hours or up to 1 month.

Holding lollipop stick, dip each cake ball into melted candy coating, letting excess drip off. Return to pan, and sprinkle with pecans. Let stand until candy coating hardens completely. Store in airtight containers for up to 3 days.

MAKES ABOUT 3 DOZEN

1 (16.5-ounce) box spice cake mix*
½ (8-ounce) package cream cheese, softened
¼ cup butter, softened
1½ cups confectioners' sugar
¼ cup apple butter
4 dozen lollipop sticks
1 (24-ounce) package vanilla-flavored candy coating, melted according to package directions
1 cup finely chopped pecans

*We used Duncan Hines Spice Cake Mix.

Shortbread Brownie Squares

CRUST
3 cups all-purpose flour
³⁄4 cup sugar
¹⁄8 teaspoon salt
1 cup butter, softened

BROWNIES
1 cup butter
6 ounces semisweet chocolate, chopped
1¹⁄2 cups sugar
5 large eggs
1 tablespoon vanilla extract
2 cups all-purpose flour
¹⁄4 cup unsweetened cocoa powder
¹⁄2 teaspoon baking powder
1¹⁄2 cups semisweet chocolate chunks

Preheat oven to 350°. Line a 13x9-inch baking pan with foil. Spray with cooking spray.

CRUST In a medium bowl, combine flour, sugar, and salt. Using a pastry blender, cut in butter until mixture is crumbly. Press mixture firmly into prepared pan. Bake for 18 to 20 minutes or until golden brown.

BROWNIES In a medium saucepan, combine butter and chopped chocolate. Cook over low heat, stirring occasionally, until chocolate is melted and smooth. Remove from heat, and let cool slightly.

In a large bowl, beat sugar and eggs with a mixer at medium-high speed until fluffy. Beat in vanilla.

In a medium bowl, combine flour, cocoa, and baking powder. Gradually add to sugar mixture, beating until combined. Add butter mixture, beating until smooth. Stir in chocolate chunks. Spoon batter over prepared crust. Bake for 35 to 40 minutes or until center is set. Let cool completely. Cut into 1¹⁄2-inch squares.

Christmas waves a magic wand over this world, and behold, everything is softer and more beautiful.

–NORMAN VINCENT PEALE

Truffled Goat Cheese Wafers

In the work bowl of a food processor, combine flour and next 4 ingredients. Pulse until mixture resembles fine crumbs. Add half-and-half and, if desired, truffle oil; process until mixture forms a ball.

Divide dough into 2 equal portions. Form each portion into a 9-inch log, and wrap tightly in plastic wrap. Chill for 8 hours or up to 24 hours. (If storing longer than 24 hours without baking, freeze dough. Let thaw in refrigerator before slicing.)

Preheat oven to 325°. Line baking sheets with parchment paper. Cut logs into 1/4-inch-thick slices. Place on prepared pans.

Bake for 14 to 16 minutes or until edges are lightly browned. Let cool on pans for 5 minutes. Remove from pans, and let cool completely on wire racks. Store in airtight containers for up to 2 days.

MAKES ABOUT 6 DOZEN

2 cups all-purpose flour
1 (8-ounce) log goat cheese, crumbled
1 3/4 cups shredded white Cheddar cheese
10 tablespoons cold butter, cubed
3/4 teaspoon seasoned salt
3 tablespoons half-and-half
1/2 teaspoon truffle oil (optional)

A bowl of fresh fruit such as apples or oranges is a simple way to welcome guests. Clove studded oranges or lemons can also be a fragrant touch. And, there is always the nice cinnamon smell coming from spiced tea or candles.

–PHYLLIS HOFFMAN DEPIANO

S'more-Caramel Popcorn

MAKES 8½ QUARTS

1 cup popcorn kernels
1 cup butter
2 cups firmly packed
   brown sugar
½ cup light corn syrup
1 teaspoon salt
1 teaspoon baking soda
1 (10-ounce) bag
   miniature
   marshmallows
6 cups honey graham
   cereal*
6 ounces chocolate-
   flavored candy
   coating, melted
   according to package
   directions

*We used Golden Honey
Graham Cereal.

Pop popcorn kernels according to package directions, omitting butter and salt. Place in a large disposable roasting pan.

Preheat oven to 200°.

In a medium saucepan, bring butter, brown sugar, corn syrup, and salt to a boil over medium-high heat. Boil for 5 minutes, stirring frequently. Remove from heat, and stir in baking soda. Pour mixture over popped corn, stirring gently to coat. Bake for 1 hour, stirring every 15 minutes.

Spread popcorn in a single layer on parchment paper. Let cool completely.

Add marshmallows and cereal to popcorn, stirring to combine. Drizzle with melted candy coating. Let stand until firm. Store in airtight containers for up to 2 weeks.

White Chocolate Hazelnut Candy Cups

Line 36 miniature muffin cups with paper liners.

In a medium bowl, combine butter, chocolate-hazelnut spread, crushed pretzels, and confectioners' sugar.

Spoon 1 to 1½ teaspoons melted candy coating into each paper-lined muffin cup. Let cool.

Spoon about 1 teaspoon butter mixture evenly over candy coating, pressing down to completely cover candy coating. Spoon remaining melted candy coating over butter mixture to cover. Garnish with chopped hazelnuts, if desired. Let stand until candy coating is hardened. Cover and refrigerate for up to 1 week.

MAKES 3 DOZEN

¼ cup butter, softened
½ cup chocolate-hazelnut spread*
½ cup crushed pretzels
¼ cup confectioners' sugar
2 (16-ounce) packages vanilla-flavored candy coating, melted according to package directions and divided
Garnish: chopped hazelnuts

*We used Nutella.

One of the most glorious messes in the world
is the mess created in the living room
on Christmas day. Don't clean it up too quickly.

–ANDY ROONEY

Gingerbread Stocking Cookies

MAKES ABOUT 1½ DOZEN

3½ cups all-purpose flour
2 teaspoons ground ginger
2 teaspoons ground
   allspice
1 teaspoon ground cloves
1 teaspoon ground
   cinnamon
¾ teaspoon baking soda
½ teaspoon salt
½ teaspoon ground
   nutmeg
½ cup unsalted butter,
   softened
1 cup sugar
1 large egg
⅔ cup unsulfured
   molasses
1 tablespoon vanilla
   extract
Meringue Powder Icing
   (recipe follows)
Garnish: green, red, and
   white sparkling sugar

MERINGUE POWDER ICING
MAKES 2½ CUPS

¼ cup cold water
3 tablespoons meringue
   powder
2 cups confectioners' sugar
Assorted paste food
   colorings

In a medium bowl, sift together flour and next 7 ingredients.

In a large bowl, beat butter and sugar with a mixer at medium-high speed for 5 minutes or until fluffy. Add egg, molasses, and vanilla, beating until combined. Gradually add flour mixture to butter mixture, beating until combined. Divide dough in half, and wrap each half in plastic wrap; chill for at least 2 hours or overnight.

Preheat oven to 350°. Line 2 baking sheets with parchment paper.

On a lightly floured surface, roll dough to ¼-inch thickness. Using a 4-inch stocking cookie cutter, cut dough, rerolling scraps as necessary. Place cookies about 1 inch apart on prepared pans. Bake for 8 to 12 minutes or until edges are just beginning to brown. (Time varies for baking rounds or stockings.) Let cool on pans for 2 minutes. Remove from pans, and let cool completely on wire racks. Frost cookies with Meringue Powder Icing, and decorate with sparkling sugar as desired.

MERINGUE POWER ICING In a medium bowl, whisk ¼ cup cold water and meringue powder until foamy. Gradually add confectioners' sugar, whisking until smooth. Add enough food coloring to achieve desired colors. Paint cookies using small pastry brushes.

Buttermilk Pancakes with Cranberry-Pear Syrup

In a large bowl, whisk together flour, sugar, baking soda, and salt. In a separate small bowl, whisk together buttermilk, butter, egg, and vanilla. Add buttermilk mixture to flour mixture; stir until just combined.

Lightly grease a nonstick skillet, and place over medium heat. Lightly grease a 3-inch round stainless steel ring. Pour approximately 1/4 cup batter into ring. Cook for approximately 6 to 8 minutes or until batter begins to bubble on the surface. Carefully remove ring, and flip pancake. Cook for approximately 5 more minutes or until lightly browned. Repeat with remaining batter, cleaning and spraying ring as necessary.

Serve with Cranberry-Pear Syrup or your own favorite syrup. Garnish with whipped cream and mint.

CRANBERRY-PEAR SYRUP In a small saucepan, combine cranberries, pear nectar, water, sugar, and honey. Cook over medium heat, stirring often, for approximately 20 minutes; cool slightly. In the container of an electric blender, add cranberry mixture. Pulse until smooth; strain, discarding solids. Use immediately, or store in an airtight container for up to 1 week.

MAKES 4 SERVINGS OR
12 (3-INCH) PANCAKES

- 1¼ **cups self-rising flour**
- 1 **tablespoon sugar**
- ¼ **teaspoon baking soda**
- ¼ **teaspoon salt**
- 1 **cup whole buttermilk**
- 2 **tablespoons melted unsalted butter**
- 1 **large egg, lightly beaten**
- ½ **teaspoon vanilla extract**
- 1 **recipe Cranberry-Pear Syrup (recipe follows)**
- **Garnish: whipped cream, fresh mint**

CRANBERRY-PEAR SYRUP
MAKES ABOUT 2 CUPS

- 1 **(10-ounce) package frozen cranberries, thawed**
- ¾ **cup pear nectar**
- ½ **cup water**
- ¼ **cup sugar**
- ¼ **cup honey**

Baked Eggs

MAKES 4 SERVINGS

4 large eggs
4 teaspoons Marsala,
  divided
4 teaspoons half-and-half,
  divided
1½ tablespoons
  unsalted butter,
  softened and divided
¾ teaspoon salt,
  divided
¾ teaspoon ground
  black pepper, divided
Garnish: fresh tarragon

Preheat oven to 350°. Generously grease 4 (4-ounce) ramekins. Crack 1 egg into each ramekin. Place 1 teaspoon Marsala and 1 teaspoon half-and-half into each ramekin. Dot each egg with 1 teaspoon butter. Evenly sprinkle each egg with salt and pepper. Bake for 10 to 12 minutes, or until desired degree of doneness. Remove from oven; cool for 5 minutes. Garnish with fresh tarragon, if desired.

Brown Sugar-Pecan Bacon

MAKES 4 SERVINGS

1 (16-ounce) package
  thick-cut bacon
½ cup firmly packed
  light brown sugar
½ cup finely ground
  pecans

Preheat oven to 400°. Line a baking sheet with aluminum foil; lightly spray with nonstick cooking spray. Place bacon on prepared baking sheet. In a small bowl, combine sugar and pecans. Rub sugar mixture over top of bacon slices, gently pressing to adhere. Bake for 20 to 25 minutes. Remove from oven; cool for 5 minutes.

Serve buttermilk pancakes with Cranberry Pear-Syrup (page 127) or purchase your favorite maple syrup. For something a little more sweet, try a caramel dessert topping.

Christmas Morning Citrus Juice

In a gallon-size pitcher, combine orange juice, pineapple juice, and mango nectar, stirring to combine. Chill or serve immediately.

MAKES ABOUT 2½ QUARTS

4 cups fresh orange juice
3 cups pineapple juice
3 cups mango nectar

Advent Calendar

Advent calendars come in many styles and types. You might like to create your own, as long as you have 25 pockets or tie-on spots for each day. Rolled printouts of poems such as *The Night Before Christmas*, by Clement Clarke Moore or songs like *White Christmas* are nice. Or you might choose a small wrapped chocolate Santa or spicy nut mix. For children, a top, marbles, small bath toy or animal figures are nice. If you use a tie-on calendar, use striped mints or candy canes.

Recipe Index

At Christmas, I am always struck by how the spirit of togetherness lies also at the heart of the Christmas story. A young mother and a dutiful father with their baby were joined by poor shepherds and visitors from afar. They came with their gifts to worship the Christ child.

–QUEEN ELIZABETH II